Unbridled
Joy

*To Joel Fishbein,
in warm friendship —*

Unbridled Joy

The Verse of Joy Skilmer

By

Lyn Nofziger

MND Publishing, Inc.

Printed in the United States of America.

MND PUBLISHING, INC.
573 Marina Road, Deatsville, Alabama 36022

Publisher's Cataloging-in-Publication Data:

Nofziger, Lyn.
    Unbridled Joy : the verse of Joy Skilmer / by
Lyn Nofziger. – 1ˢᵗ ed.
    p. cm.
    LCCN: 99-76226
    ISBN: 0-940847132

    1.   Politicians–United States–Poetry.
    2. Celebrities–United States–Poetry.   I. Title.

PS3564.O34U63 2000   811'.6
                 QB199-1963

For Margaret,
without whose enthusiasm, hard work
and encouragement this little book would
never have seen the light of day.

"... the rhyme scheme – *ab*, *ab*, ad infinitum; and the meter – iambic two-syllables-short-of-pentameter – was easy stuff to play with so I kept writing the darn things as the muse, Erato, I believe, struck me."   —J.S.

Contents:

Preface

A fund-raising project aimed at wealthy donors to Ronald Reagan's presidential library was the inspiration for the bits of verse in this little book.

The library fundraisers came up with the idea of planting a grove of flowering crab apple trees on the slopes around the library which sits on a hilltop overlooking the Simi Valley on one side and the Pacific Ocean in the distance. Each tree would be sold for a mere ten thousand dollars.

It was a fine idea and I'm sure raised and continues to raise substantial sums for the library. But it was a little rich, not so much for my blood as for my checkbook. The same is true for hundreds, nay thousands, of other Reagan supporters.

Therefore, in lieu of purchasing a tree I wrote the initial poem. The others followed naturally as occasions arose and individuals inspired.

They are printed herein, dear reader, for what I earnestly hope will be your enjoyment.

Joy Skilmer
January, 2000

This is where it all began — J.S.

Trees II

I think that I shall never see
A ten thousand dollar Reagan tree,
A tree that may in autumn wear
Leaves that look like Reagan's hair,
A tree that thinks of Ron all day
And hopes he'll never go away,
Upon whose bosom snow's not lain
'Cause all you get out there is rain.

    Poems are made by folks like me
    Too poor to buy a Reagan tree.

A Chinese Trie

I think that I shall never see
A Chinese crook like Charlie Trie,
A Trie who once brought bags of bills
To help with Bill's financial ills,
Who went to White House fund events,
Gave lots of bucks, showed little sense,
A Trie who knew Bill could be bought
And worked at it til he got caught,
A Trie who may next summer wear
Striped prison clothes, eat prison fare.
   Poems are made by fools like me,
   Just thankful we're not Charlie Trie.

The Dress

I think that I shall never see
Miss Monica on bended knee.
When she kneels down by night or day
You can be sure it's not to pray.
Bill said to her, "To prove I care
I've sent a dress for you to wear.
And if we ever meet again
Make sure it does not get a stain."

    Poems are made by fools like me,
    But we don't write on bended knee.

Vernon J

I thought that I would never see
Ol' Vernon Jordan up a tree.
I thought he was too smart by far
To ride with Monica in a car
And find for her a lawyer guy
Who'd tell her how to testify,
Or stick his neck way out for Bill
And still refuse the beans to spill.
Though Vernon is Bill's loyal friend
Bill will betray him in the end.

    Poems are made by fools like me,
    But not like Jordan – up a tree.

Old Jim McD

I thought that I would never see
Old Jim McDougal cop a plea.
But I sure figured he would die
Before he came to testify.
In Arkansas folks don't live long
Who sing the true Whitewater song.
So now we see why Sue won't give –
Unlike old Jim she wants to live.
She's safer in the county jail
Than telling her Whitewater tale.

    Poems are made by fools like me,
    While Jim is dead and Sue's not free.

Patrick B

I think that I shall never see
A candidate like Patrick B.
A candidate who doesn't care
If he gets in his party's hair,
A candidate who's not afraid
To stand against free foreign trade,
Who takes a stand and speaks his mind
Though it can get him in a bind,
A candidate who'd rather lose
Than read the polls, then change his views.
    If poems are made by fools like me
    Then who'll campaign for Patrick B.

Christmas Starr

I think that I shall never see
A Starr upon a Christmas tree,
'Cause if you are a Christmas star
You are a star with just one r.
But if you are a two r'd Starr
A lawyer then is what you are
And not a Christmas ornament
Unless you get the president.
But if that happens you can bet
Ken Starr will shine the brightest yet.

    Poems are made by fools like me
    Who wish two r's shone from the tree.

Bill Clinton Speaks:

I thought that I would never see

Kathleen Willey rat on me.

For after all this boy from Hope

Certainly deserved a grope.

And while it's true I copped a feel,

It's also true we had a deal.

She'd hide the fact that I'm a slob

And in return she'd get a job.

    Poems are made by many fools

    While I ignore both rhymes and rules.

The Testimony

I think that I shall never see
Slick Will before a grand jury
Testifying just what was done
When he and Monica had their fun
Or that he'd told her, "Tell a lie
If you are called to testify."
He'd have to feel a bit of dread
Not knowing what some others said.
Vernon Jordan, Betty Currie–
What did they say to the grand jury?

    Poems are made by fools like me
    Waiting for Bill's testimony.

Wen Ho Lee

The thing that's amazing to me
Is the story of Wen Ho Lee,
A brilliant scientific guy
And probably a Chinese spy
Working for the Red Chinese
And stealing secrets with great ease
From underneath our very nose
At super secret Alamos.
Though Clinton says, "You can't blame me,"
He's on the take from the Red Chinee.
What's his excuse when they come back
The day the Red Chinese attack.
      But still there's one thing puzzles me –
      Why is Wen Ho still running free?

Lies

I think that I shall never see

A man who lies like Slick Willie.

He lies when truth would serve him best.

He lies in anger and in jest.

He lies about his scores in games.

He lies about his scores with dames.

He takes an oath and then he lies.

He won't admit, he just denies.

He lies or claims, "I don't recall."

He hardly tells the truth at all.

    If hell is for those folks who lie

    Then you can bet Bill's going to fry.

The Traveler

I thought that I would never see
Bill Clinton from his country flee
And fly off to a foreign shore
(For after all there is no war)
To visit countries of no worth,
The darkest spots upon this earth,
To get away from sin and shame,
To get away from every dame
Who claims he groped or dropped his pants
Or made some other lewd advance.
    Some poems are made by fools (alas!)
    Who'd rather rhyme than make a pass.

The Candidates

I thought that I would never see
So many in the GOP
Who say or hint it's their intent
Next time to run for president.
At least a dozen, or a score
All want to challenge Albert Gore.
The trouble is that not one has
The slightest bit of real pizzazz.
Their dullness runs from pole to pole,
From young George Bush to Liddy Dole.

    While poems are made by fools like me
    It's God must help the GOP.

Paula

I thought that I would never see

Paula Jones in misery,

Unhappy that her civil suit

By Susan Wright was rendered moot.

Has Paula Jones now lost her chance

To prove that Bill once dropped his pants

And asked her for a special kiss,

One that would bring him special bliss?

Her one last hope is to appeal.

Bet, if she wins, you'll hear Bill squeal.

    Poems are made by fools like me

    While Paula plans a higher plea.

South of the Border

I thought I'd never see Slick Willie
Take a trip clear down to Chile
To meet with all those Latin leadahs
And grope their lovely senoritas.
Of senoritas there are plenty
To flock around El Presidente.
I thought that Bill might stay at home
And let his eyes and fingers roam,
Instead of flying down to Chile
To find a willing Latin filly.

    Poems are made by fools like me
    While Bill still cheats on Hillary.

The Big Giver

I think that I shall never see

Someone so lacking charity

As Albert Gore, Bill Clinton's veep,

Whose name so rightly rhymes with "cheap,"

Who gives amounts that are so small

He might as well not give at all.

Though he likes nuns to grease his palms

He hates the thought of giving alms.

And so we find a buck a day

Is all that he will give away.

    One thing Al Gore just won't believe:

    It's better to give than to receive.

Cigs and Taxes

I thought that I would never see
Tobacco as a money tree,
Or kiddies used just as a way
To make tobacco smokers pay
For social programs Dems espouse
To help them to win back the House.
I thought that I would never see
So many in the GOP
Who claim to want big gov't to ax
But still support the smokers tax.
    Poems are made by folks like me.
    The fools are in the GOP.

Newt Blows

I think that I may never know
What finally made Newt Gingrich blow.
I'll never know just what it took
For Newt to call Slick Will a crook,
Or to assert he's gone too far
By tossing smears at Kenny Starr.
Do polls he has show Bill's a knave?
Could that be why he's gotten brave?
Or does this mean it's his intent
To make a run for president?
    I wish I knew why Newt is doing
    Things he was 'til now eschewing.

Stonewall Clinton

I never thought, I could not guess
How well Bill could stonewall the press,
That he is such an agile dancer
He could evade and never answer
Any question that he might get
About his favorite nymphette.
I never thought that I would see
Bill dodge and dance so nimble–y
He has surviv'ed every test
And proved he is the very best.
    Poems are made by fools like me
    Who can't stonewall like Slick Willie.

The Give Away

I thought I'd never see the day
A president would give away
Our best defense technologies
To people like the Red Chinese.
Even though Bill dodged the draft
And surely is involved in graft
Within my mind there was no doubt
He would not sell our country out.
But I was wrong as I could be –
Bill's been bought by the Red Chinee.

    Poems are made by fools like me
    While Bill consorts with the enemy.

Tiennamen Square

I though that I would never see
Proof Bill was bought by the Red Chinee.
I thought that he would never dare
To greet them in Tiennamen Square.
I thought he might recall the dead
Who for freedom their blood shed,
Crushed by tanks in the place where
Bill pays his debts – Tiennamen Square.
What kind of man just doesn't care
About the blood in Tiennamen Square?

    Poems are made by fools like me
    Who've not been bought by the Red Chinee.

Bombs for All

I thought the day would never come
When India would have the bomb
And Pakistan would build one, too.
Now who'll tell Clinton what to do?
He's settled now for talking tough,
But all the world knows it's a bluff,
For he who dodged his country's call
Can hardly be believed at all.
And we may learn on some day soon
Bill dances just to China's tune.

    So though this world with bombs is cursed.
    Fear not! Bill will surrender first.

The Zhu

National Zoo is great, it's true
But China also has its Zhu.
Our zoo's a place where monkeys play.
Their Zhu gives the dough away
To Willie Clinton and Algore,
Who'll happily sell out the store
To help them their elections win.
For taking bribes to them's no sin,
Though what they give for what they get
Is used to build Zhu's missile threat.
    But that's a chance the boys must take
    When it's the White House that's at stake.

Mumps

Sweet Chelsea must be in the dumps
To learn her daddy had the mumps
When he was just a little lad.
That fact can hardly make her glad.
Now she wonders who's her father –
"Tell me, Mom, unless you'd rather
That I go on pretending he
Is still the dad he claims to be.
Is 'Nita lying or was dad?
Do I have reason to be sad?"

    "Daughter! Daughter! Indeed you do.
    What ALL those women say is true!"

The New Houdini

I think the day will never come
When Congress will impeach the bum.
The Dems, for sure, just won't give in
'Cause all they want to do is win.
And though the GOP tut-tuts,
Impeach him? No! They've not the guts
In the Senate? Oh, happy day!
The house should make this all go 'way.
Then Bill gets off, he goes scot free,
Despite what Starr's shown him to be.
    So though the Dems claim Starr's a meanie,
    Bill proves that he's the new Houdini.

The Impeach Tree

I think that I will never see
Bill Clinton in an impeach tree,
A tree whose fruit is Clinton's lies
That to high crimes may sometimes rise,
A tree that may in campaigns wear
Red Chinese money in her hair,
A tree whose branches give the shade
For Bill to duck and dodge, evade,
A tree that knows that he can win
Just by confessing mortal sin.
    Poems are made by fools like me
    Who once thought Bill was up a tree.

The Disciple

Whoever thought Algore would learn
From Bill just how the truth to spurn.
Or that he'd learn to tell great lies
That make Bill's look like humble pies.
Our Bill would never claim to be
"Love Story's" hero or that he
Hates tobacco, but not disdain
To take their dough for his campaign.
Nor would he say, not on a bet,
He invented the Internet.

    Algore, like Bill, for truth don't care,
    But he's not got Bill's savoire faire.

The Story of Algore

How well I remember Algore,
The fellow was always a bore,
But his record of achieving
Is beyond all believing.

      * * *

A hero first in a novel
Up from his birth in a hovel.
(Or was it the Fairfax Hotel?
Whatever... He ended up well.)
Then, to his wondrous contention –
"The Internet's my invention."
And thence to the slopping of hogs,
Plowing the hills, draining the bogs,
Cutting the hay, killing the goose,
Growing tobacco, fighting its use.
Then living up to Bill's intent
By reinventing government.

      * * *

Man of the people, Albert Gore,
As president he'll do much more.
Win or lose, it's clear as can be,
Algore is Clinton's legacy.

In Old Virginny

Say what you will about George Allen,
A pint of him is worth a gallon
Of Democrat senator Robb,
Who started good but's now a slob.
He started right but then moved left,
Leaving conservatives bereft.
He backs Bill Clinton all the way,
Supports him both at work and play,
Betrays us all with every vote.
Let's shove George Allen down his throat
    Virginia voters have one job
    It's getting rid of Chucky Robb.

Limericks

Chortled Bill Clinton with a grin,
"When the trial's all over we win.
For it isn't the right
That carries the fight,
It's the party that's best with the spin."

* * *

Things in the White House are chilly
T'wixt Hillary and Slick Willie.
It comes down to this–
It was more than a kiss
Bill got from that loving young filly.

* * *

"Defending Bill Clinton is tough,"
Said a savvy old lawyer named Ruff
"He tells us more lies
Than a barn full of flies
For Clinton enough's not enough."

* * *

The White House is every pol's goal.
But to get there really takes soul –
Or the ability to fake it.
And most never make it.
Ask Humphrey or Mondale or Dole.

More Limericks

The Democrats have a big grudge
Against that young fellow named Drudge
'Cause he's not afraid
To publish their grade
Whenever it seems that they fudge.

* * *

Bob Dole had a great lot of hustle
And could flex his political muscle.
Though he never made president
He did well for a resident
Of a small Kansas town named Russell.

* * *

Bill Clinton is nothing, I fear,
If he isn't, at least, sincere.
He says wrong is right
And noonday is night
And expects you'll believe what you hear.

* * *

A bald Clinton pal named Carville
Declared, "Starr makes me real ill.
He's pickin' on Bill
And chasin' sweet Hil.
Get even? You bet that we will."

Raising Money Limericks

Honest Abe looked down from the sky,
Said, "Clinton's a sleazy young guy.
He rented my bed
At thousands a head –
Then defends what he did with a lie.

* * *

"Money that we raised by the ton,"
Said Clinton, "is the reason we won.
We gave coffees galore
Rented rooms and much more,
Such as briefings on Air Force One."

* * *

"The White House is never for sale,"
Cried Bill Clinton, turning real pale.
"I've rented it, true,
To a fat cat or two
But for that you can't send me to jail."

* * *

Gore's asking for dough on the phone
Is something we may not condone
But in Congress' halls
They make similar calls.
The veep is in no way alone.

Algore Limericks

If you want to meet a real bore
There's none like our veep, Al Gore.
He has nothing to say
In a very dull way.
So be glad he doesn't say more.

* * *

Not only is Albert Gore
An A-one, first class bore
But the gaffes he's made
Put Quayle in the shade
By a ratio of fourteen to four.

* * *

The ethical vice president
Told the press, "I am innocent.
If I broke any laws
It was for a just cause
And without any evil intent."

* * *

A vice president named Al Gore
On a stack of Bibles he swore
He didn't know it was mon
He got from the nun
Who lurked at the Buddhist's church door.

Feeling Glad

I know it's wrong of me to smile
At the thought of Clinton's trial.
For properly I should feel sad.
But, far from that, I'm feeling glad.
It's worth to me at least a tuppence
If Slick Will gets his comeuppance.
That I'd pay, in fact, and more
To see them show Slick Will the door.
The senate must it's duty do
And if it won't I'm gonna sue.
   But in my heart I know that I
   Will get my wish when fat pigs fly.

Impeach!

I thought that Bill would never reach
A point when folks would cry, "Impeach!"
I thought that he might slither by
Without a public hue and cry,
Like he has done so many times,
As folks ignored his petty crimes
And sighed and looked the other way.
"That's just our Bill," you'd hear them say.
But "just our Bill" today won't fly.
They've learned their Bill's one slimy guy.

    So now they cry, "Impeach! Impeach!"
    While Bill still hopes he's out of reach.

Three Cheers for Susan Wright

Three cheers! Three cheers for Susan Wright
Who recognized that Bill's a blight
On honor, truth and honesty
And, yes, the court's integrity.
"Civil contempt," Judge Susan said
And heaped it on Bill's hoary head.
She did not call Slick Will a liar,
Just said that he's a falsifier.
But make it clear they mean the same.
She's a tough and gutsy dame
To nail the shameless one this way.
Judge Susan, you have made my day.
  If the senate had men like you
  Bill Clinton's day would now be through.

Take Me Out To The Ballgame

The days of dull at last are gone,

The Baseball season's coming on.

Football and hockey, basketball,

Their seasons now are looming small,

For spring has sprung, the grass has riz,

Spring training's where the action is.

Daffodils are blooming yeller.

Whatever happened to Bob Feller?

The grass upon the sward is green

And, gee, I miss old Dizzy Dean,

And Ted and Stan, the Babe and Joe

Say, where do all past seasons go?

 Don't fret. A new one's soon to start.

 Be still my rapid-beating heart.

Eager Beavers

I thought that I would never see
A beaver fell a cherry tree,
A tree whose blossoms brightly gleam
Beside the tidal basin stream,
A tree that millions yearly view
By morning sun and evening dew.
But I was wrong, those eager beavers
Wielding teeth like butchers' cleavers
Slice through their trunks like they're butter
Making all tree huggers shudder.
Especially the Japanese
Who sent us all those lovely trees.
Though beavers may hate Arbor Day
They'll not forget Pearl Harbor Day.

Poems are made by fools like me
But beavers can chop down a tree.

More Lies

I should have known that Bill would try
To con us with another lie
And claim he only lied but once.
I guess he thinks we're each a dunce,
That we'd believe so bald a lie.
Hey, Bill! That's one that did not fly.
For we recall the deposition
And the jury's inquisition.
As we heard your each denial
We knew that truth is not your style
And all the lies you've told before
Are way too many to keep score.
    If only truth will set men free
    Bill's 'prisoned for eternity.

Bill's War

Once more our Bill's decided he
Must act to change his legacy.
So now for him it's bombs away,
Begin another war today,
Let Algore fret about the burbs
While Bill stays busy killing Serbs
And proving to Milosovitch
He's a hard-nosed son of a bitch
who will not let the bombing cease
Until old Milo sues for peace.
True, we might lose a man or two.
Our Bill won't care, he'll see it through
    Poems are made by fools like me,
    While Bill works on his legacy.

Two Choices

Mayhap the press will wait in vain
For Bush to say, "I used cocaine."
But then again he may admit
"I used it just a little bit."
He finds it hard to hold his stand
When heckled by the media band.
He says, "I will not play your game,"
But plays it with them just the same.
He finds it hard as time goes by
To duck the truth but still not lie.
He has two choices: One-to stall
And learn from Clinton to stonewall.
Or, two, at last the truth to bare
And find that people just don't care.

    What e'er his choice he must decide
    Before his hide's completely fried.

Daddy Bush

I think that I will never see

A Bush as sturdy as a tree,

A Bush who on another day

His re-election kicked away,

A Bush who jumped out of a plane

To prove he had not lived in vain,

A Bush who fathered two nice boys

Who are their daddy's prides and joys.

Each ran for governor and won

Thus proving each his daddy's son.

    And like their dad each one's hell bent

    Some day to be our president.

The Cigar

I think that Bill has gone too far

With what he does with a cigar.

Tobacco's made–I am not joking–

For dipping, chewing or for smoking.

And shouldn't be us`ed for inserting

As a follow-up to flirting.

We know that kids shouldn't smoke the weed,

But Bill's a nasty kid indeed

To stoop to pulling such a trick

On a dumb and lovelorn chick.

 One thing we know, and that's enough:

 This president's not up to snuff.

New Year's

New Year's comes but once a year–
When I was young I drank my cheer.
When we toasted "Old Lang Syne"
I downed the gin and not the wine,
Then double lines I followed home,
Despite the fuzz that fuzzed my dome.
But as I older, smarter grew
The toasts I drank were smaller, few.
And now when New Year's comes, instead
Of drinking toasts, I'm snug in bed.

    Hey! Moms against the drink and drive,
    Sober I am, and still alive.

So Long Newt

I thought I'd never see the day
When Newt Gingrich would go away,
When because he had a squeaker
He would quit his job as Speaker.
Four years ago his finest hour
Brought the GOP to power.
The bombs he threw had done the job,
As with the Dems they played real hob.
But when he took the Speaker's role
He put his party in the hole.

    Oft men who spark rebellions find
    Peace must demand another kind

Ode to Henry Hyde

I'm glad some folks are on my side,
And one of those is Henry Hyde,
Old Henry Hyde who loves the law.
Who holds the senate not in awe,
Who looks his foes square in the eye
And charges Clinton with the lie,
Who tells the Senate, "Do what's right,"
Who's not afraid to join the fight,
Who won't stand for diminution
Of our nation's constitution.
    Poems are made by fools like me
    While men like Henry keep us free.

The Misunderstanding

I thought I'd never live to see
A brouhaha o'er "niggardly."
Or have the brothers make a fuss
'Cause it was used by a white cuss.
Though it only means "tight-fisted"
That white boy should have resisted
Saying a word that eas'ly could
And eas'ly was misunderstood,
Should have known some would complain,
Apology would be in vain,
Known the mayor, to prove he's black,
Would quickly give to him the sack.

    Poems are made by fools like me,
      And whitey shouldn't say "niggardly."

Our Kids

If Clinton ever hits the skids
'Twill be because of all our kids.
For their fates in straits are dire
If senators forgive the liar
And say corruption is no bar,
That he, indeed, didn't go too far,
That though his sins are manifold
He can onto his office hold.
If senators agree to this
How can we tell our kids it is
Still wrong to perjure and to lie?
"If Clinton did it so can I."

    Besides, who thinks a mere slapped wrist
    Will ever make that man desist?

Michael Jordan

And now no more we'll see the day
When Michael Jordan comes to play
There on the court of basketball
With other fellows nine feet tall,
See Michael Jordan –Hall of Fame–
Out shooting shots that win the game.
And running rings around his foes,
As well befits the pro of pros–
Perhaps the greatest ever seen,
One fellow who deserved the green.
    With Michael gone the NBA
    Should fold its tent and slink away.

That Bloomin' Blumenthal

It looks like Sidney Blumenthal,
Slick Willie's sycophant and pal,
Is in trouble just for trying
To help Bill by lying. Lying
When he said he did no talking
Concerning Monica and stalking
To his friend Chris who with loose lip,
Kind of like Ms. Linda Tripp,
Swears, though Sidney now is balking,
That Sid says Bill talked of stalking,
Said Monica just wanted sex–
The sort of thing our Bill rejects.
 Now who would lie of things like this?
 Could it be Bill, or Sid or Chris?

Willie Gets Off Free

I think that I will never know

Why the senate did not throw

Slick Willie Clinton out. I guess

That even though he'd made a mess

That would do a baby proud,

They thought that such should be allowed

For president's who feel our pain.

Therefore what's right goes down the drain

With honor and with decency.

And Willie Clinton gets off free.

    Poems are made by many fools.

    While Clinton safely breaks the rules.

Damn Lies

Bill says he's never used cocaine.

(I guess he sniffed and sniffed in vain)

He never sniffed, he didn't inhale.

(And some believe his ev'ry tale)

Roger Clinton begs to differ

Calls bro' Bill a major sniffer

Would prob'ly testify in court

That Billy C. just loved to snort

Says, "Ignore bro' Bill's demeanor.

"Nose is like a vacuum cleaner."

    So Bill has told us one more lie,

    While young George Bush is scared to try.

Leftish Both

Democrats must all feel badly

About Algore and Bill Bradley.

Two of the dullest men in town

Who hope to wear their party's crown.

Though leftish both, they're smart and deep

But both also put crowds to sleep.

Thus, some of us can hardly wait

For the Bradley/Gore debate

To see which one's the biggest bore.

Will it be Bradley or Algore?

    Whichever one's his party's choice

    Republicans can't but rejoice.

Their Lowest Hour

Now who is left who can deny
The Democrats all love the lie.
No other reason can there be
For votes that set the liar free.
It's not enough for them to say,
"We hate the lie but Bill must stay."
It's not enough that they assert,
"The lie was bad, but none were hurt."
They may excuse, they may explain.
Their lies, like his, are all in vain.

    In what may be their lowest hour
    They have traded truth for power.

The Yankee Clipper

They've buried Joe DiMaggio.
He's now beneath the ground.
But though we know he's down below
He's also heaven bound.

They've buried Joe DiMaggio.
One thing we hope is so,
That he will meet on heaven's street
His Marilyn Monroe.

They've buried Joe DiMaggio.
His death it was a shame.
But angels grin and vote him in
The Heaven Hall of Fame.

They've buried Joe DiMaggio
And Mr. Coffee, too.
But up above we know he'll love
St. Peter's better brew.

So goodbye Joe DiMaggio.
Farewell Yankee Clipper.
You've sailed away to a better day
Where you're once more young and chipper.

They've buried Joe DiMaggio.
Though it was his time to go,
As long as baseball games are played
We'll remember Joltin' Joe.

Remember Bob Dole

Who doesn't remember Bob Dole?
The White House was always his goal.
He ran for veep with Jerry Ford.
Came kind of close, but never scored.
Vied with Reagan four years later–
Should have stood in Ulan Bator,
Ran once again in ninety-six,
Couldn't match up to Clinton's tricks
Three times running, thrice in the hole.
But he's not quit, not Bobby Dole.
Sends Liddy out to head the team,
Hopes she'll fulfill his longtime dream.
What Bob couldn't do, she maybe can.
For this time out she be de man.

Dorian Gray

I wonder if Bill holds a grudge

Against that fellow, Matthew Drudge

Who peered beneath Bill's unlined face

And found, and this to our disgrace,

Inside the attic of Bill's mind

A portrait of another kind,

A picture of a man depraved,

One who by evil's all enslaved,

One that he hides from light of day–

The twisted face of Dorian Gray.

    Poems are made by fools like me,

    But Bill has fooled the whole country.

Hillary, Our Hillary

Why folks would want to pillory
Bill Clinton's bride, our Hillary,
Is something I don't understand.
Of all the babes within our land
The brightest star of which to sing,
The leftest of our land's left wing,
Who found the right's conspiracy
And lied to keep her husband free,
The greatest Yankee fan of all
Who now is waiting New York's call
(As friends and foes stand breathlessly)
Is Hillary, our Hillary.
    As Bill strives for his legacy
    He well may find it's Hillary.

Avoid the Floyd

I've always hoped I could avoid
A hurricane as big as Floyd.
It's hard to think there could occur
One that blows at 150 per,
Or one that spans a corrider
As wide as all of Florider,
Or one that rains in just one day
Enough to wash a state away,
A 'cane that just because it can,
Destroys the handiworks of man.

    Poems are made by fools like me
    While from big Floyd scared millions flee.

The Astronaut

I thought I'd never see again
A man in space named Johnny Glenn.
Once around I thought enough,
Though he was made of the right stuff.
A hero Johnny Glenn up there,
But something less when he's down here.
He did not pay his campaign debt.
For Keating aid what did he get?
In senate hearings he stonewalled.
Bribed by Clinton he really stalled.
For doing wrong Bill did him right
And gave to him his last space flight.

    Poems are made by fools like me
    Who know Glenn's not what he claims to be.

Guts?

Republicans who have some guts?

In the Senate? You must be nuts!

Yes, in the House I can believe.

For the Senate I sadly grieve.

(As opposed to joyful grieving)

It's their oaths that some are leaving.

Oaths and duty to the nation,

Any hope of real salvation.

They'll settle for a censure vote–

A bone, indeed, in honor's throat.

> When this farce at last is over
>
> We'll know which "heroes" ran for cover.

New York, New York

I wonder if there'll ever be
A senator named Hillary,
A senator from old New York,
Doling out the federal pork.
I wonder if she wants to run
Because she knows her husband's done.
I wonder if she thinks she's meant
Some day to be our president
And senator is just step one
Before she makes the major run.

> How long? How long before we find
> What's lurking in her devious mind?

Boo–Hoo

Don't think that there will ever be
Any return to normalcy
Within the nation's politics
Since Bill escaped his latest fix.
For Democrats now clearly think
The GOP is at the brink
And they can win the Congress back
With one continuous attack.
So watch, as daily down the road
The Dems unloose a heavy load.
And watch while Bill pulls up his pants
And deftly leads the Dem's advance.
    And all Republicans will do
    Is whine, complain and cry "Boo-hoo."

Another Day For Johnny K

So Johnny Kasich, bless his heart,

Has wisened up and gotten smart.

And thus it is, the mailman's son

Has now decided not to run

For president – his first intent

He found to be it was not meant.

He took one look at young George Bush

And then decided, "What's the rush?

George has the money and the men.

My time will come around again.

If next year brings us Albert Gore

There always is two thousand, four

And if I have to I can wait

To make my run in aught aught eight.

    I've changed the time but not my goal.

    This year I'll leave to Forbes and Dole.

The Kennedy Curse

I feel compelled to write this verse

About the Kennedys' great curse.

It is no curse that leaves them dead.

Since all men die. The curse instead

Has been inflicted on just one--

 Father Joe's last living son.

He's lived to see three brothers die.

Two sisters in their graves now lie.

Three nephews, too, for now John-john

Is listed with the ones who've gone

    The curse on Ted – he's doomed to be

    The one last living Kennedy

Kosovo

I think that I don't want to know
About that place called Kosovo,
Or why them folks is fightin' there.
Don't want to know and little care.
It ain't my fault they want to fight
It ain't my fault they ain't too bright.
We had folks here, some mountain boys
Knowed as the Hatfields and McCoys
Who thought it right to shoot and kill.
In Kosovo they think that still.
Them Balkanites just love to feud.
Don't care if we-uns think 'em rude.

    So let 'em fight, is what I say
    It ain't our fight, not any way.

The Lie Lovers

I think that I would like to see
The guy who said truth sets you free
And say to him, to his surprise,
That freedom also comes from lies.
Slick Willie C. has made it plain
That lies may not be all in vain,
That perjury and oaths ignored,
That are by decent folks abhorred,
Will pass, as even fools have guessed,
The Democratic honor test,

> Poems are made by such as I,
> But Democrats all love the lie.

Gun Control

If they put gunlocks on each gun
Then what will Junior do for fun?
Will he feel blue, will he feel sad
Because he can't shoot mom and dad,
Because he can't go off to school
And violate the "no guns" rule?
And when a child goes off half-cocked
What will he do when guns are locked?
When Junior cannot use a gun
Will he be nice to everyone?

    Not our Junior – here's the rub.
    He'll just resort to knife or club.

Season's Greetings

T'was the day before Christmas and all through the town

Republicans smiled while Dems wore a frown.

Censure it seems was just out of reach

As Reps in the House had voted "impeach."

One after one they had voted new grief

For Billy Jeff Clinton, the Liar-in-Chief.

Hyde and DeLay, the conservative clan

Had stood up to Bill. Yes, man after man

Had paid no attention to Democrat bluster

And bravely, one time, had finally passed muster.

So, hurrah for the Reps and down with Slick Will

Whose present this year is a large, bitter pill.

This verse must be short; I've run out of time

And it's not always easy to find a good rhyme.

So I end it with this: To Republicans, "Good Cheer.

Merry Christmas to all and a Happy New Year."

Nixon's Men

And so we'll never see again
Another one of Nixon's men.
John Ehrlichman has now gone west
To meet out there with all the rest –
Bryce Harlow who was best of all
And was not one who took a fall.
John Mitchell, Nixon's firmest friend,
Like many more has reached the end.
Bob Haldeman, Dick Nixon's chief,
Whose loyalty brought him to grief,
Bob Finch and Maury Stanns have died
And passed on to the other side.
And Nixon? He is out there, too,
Watching as his men come through,
Waiting in, as they pass it by,
The Oval Office in the sky.

 And still they wish, though it's too late,
 They'd never heard of Watergate.

The Splendid Splinter

Though Joe DiMaggio is dead
For baseball fans there still is Ted.
While Joe did not survive the winter
We still have "The Splendid Splinter."
The greatest hitter of them all
Has yet to heed death's final call.
The Yankee Clipper's sailed away
But Williams lives another day
Though in his prime Joe got his licks,
T'was Teddy batted four-oh-six.
    Though each one's in the Hall of Fame
    There's still just one "Teddy Ballgame."

The FALN

When a FALN who's a felon
Is turned loose, something is smellin'.
From the White House there's a stink
Caused by the Bill and FALN link.
When those terrorists went free
Did Clinton act so Hillary.
Would get a bigger Rican vote
And be a bone in Rudy's throat?
Republicans think this is so.
But for sure they'd like to know.
But it won't happen, just no way
Bill tells them, "Take a hike today."

> Bill seldom heeds the Congress' call
> Because he's found he can stonewall.

To Janet R

I thought I'd never see the day
When Janet Reno went astray.
And to her oath would not be true
By plain , flatout refusing to
Name independent counsel for
Our lying veep, old Albert Gore.
Old Albert Gore, like Bill, forsooth,
Would rather lie than tell the truth
And Reno keeps her job just by
Defending Algore's right to lie.

    Poems are made by fools like me
    While Jan makes sure that Al stays free.

Winter in DC

I thought that I would never know
A DC winter without snow,
A winter that just once or twice
Dropped a wee bit of snow or ice,
A winter that most ev'ry day
Forced all the kiddies out to play
Without their sleds or skis or skates,
Or even caps to warm their pates.
A winter more like spring or fall,
A winter that was not at all.
>Though some may cheer when north winds blow,
>God bless those days when there's no snow.

Things are Going the Way I Like

Things are going the way I like:
Kevorkian's on a hunger strike,
While in contempt Slick Will's been found
(Let credit to Judge Wright resound.)
And Kenny Starr now would redact
The Independent Counsel Act.
And when it comes to Kosovo
More folks are shouting, "We won't go!"
They think like Bill thought once before,
"It's not our problem, not our war."
And Algore's working without fail
To try to out-gaffe Danny Quayle.

    To top it off the year's at spring,
    And thus the joyous song I sing.

Fact or Fiction

Edmund Morris, how can it be
That in your new biography
Of Ronald Reagan you couldn't resist
Using a person who doesn't exist,
Mixing fiction in with fact,
Making it somehow less exact,
Making us wonder what is true,
What Reagan did or did not do,
What did he say, what was he like
When he was grown or just a tike?
There's now no way that we can know
What is fiction and what is so.
    Hark now to the critics' chorus,
    "You wrote it wrong, Edmund Morris."

The Independent Counsel Law

The Independent Counsel Law,
Once held by many men in awe
And filled so many more with dread
Has now expired, now is dead.
But yet today at a hearing
On its abuses I was cheering
Those who came to testify
How they were willing to defy
The tyrant hand of government.
Each one stood firm and never bent.
So sound the klaxon, blow the bugle
For Mike Espy and Sue McDougal
For Julie Steele and all the rest
Who never blinked but met the test.
    It's folks like these, who do not give,
    Bring hope to all, make freedom live.

At Last

And so at last we finally know,
Because Miss Hillary told us so,
Just what it is makes Bill a liar,
Poltroon, cheat and falsifier,
Why still he hops from bed to bed
Or asks for oral sex instead.
We know now why he dodged the draft
And sold out for some Chinese graft.
We know now why he didn't inhale
And let Web Hubbell go to jail.
Hillary says he's not to blame
The fault it lies (and oh, the shame)
With his ma and grandma who,
Arguing till the air turned blue,

    In front of Bill when only four,
    Twisted his life forever more.

Defining Moments in History

Caesar sat with his toga on
Contemplating how things had gone.
Then, though fate looked mighty sticky,
"Veni," he cried, and "vidi, vici,"
And promptly crossed the Rubicon.

George Washington pulled at his hair
Said to himself, "But do I dare
To attack the Hessians tonight
And risk it all in one big fight?"
Then went and crossed the Delaware.

Abraham Lincoln, mighty brave,
Saved the union, freed the slave
Was out one night to celebrate
When John Booth shot him in the pate
And sent him to an early grave.

The Indians feared that they were through,
But Sitting Bull rallied the Sioux.
Took on the white man's whole army
And won the fight at Wounded Knee,
Scalped George Custer and all his crew.

Eisenhower took a chance
Sent his soldiers off to France
Landed them in Normandy
Marched them through to Germany
And kicked the Axis in the pants.

Ronnie Reagan, full of fire,
Attacked the Soviet Empire.
Said, "Their evil's not for me."
Vowed to make the world free,
And helped the Communists expire.

Bill Clinton, finger wagging, said,
"I never took that girl to bed."
Then sought to build a legacy
Of greatness, but t'was not to be.
His legacy's the lie instead.

Defining Moments in History II

Eve plucked the apple from the tree.
"Eat it, Babe. It'll set you free,"
Said the serpent, all beguiling.
As she ate it he was smiling;
Knew what he'd done to you and me.

Caesar strolling down the iter
Heard Brutus' feet – patter, pitter,
Ere he could turn he'd lost his life
"Cause Brutus stuck him with his knife.
If Caesar lived he'd still be bitter.

Columbus thought the world was round,
Then figured India he had found
He was wrong but that is best.
Because he dared to sail out west
We live today on freedom's ground.

Benedict Arnold got real mad.
He thought that he'd been treated bad,
Thought he should be treated greater,
When he wasn't he turned traitor.
How sad! How sad! How very sad!

Teddy Kennedy, having fun
Stepped on the gas, gave it the gun
Ran off the bridge; the girl drowned.
When it was over Teddy found
Too late, he'd never be the one.

Lyndon Johnson got in a jam
By sending troops to Vietnam
Later on was heard to mutter,
"We can have both guns and butter,"
Then chickened out, went on the lam.

Mikhail Gorbachev, standing tall,
Thought with Reagan he'd have a ball,
Would eat his lunch at Reykjavik,
Made some threats; they did not stick,
And in the end tore down the wall.

Sue McD

Sue McDougal went off to jail
'Cause she refused to tattletale
 On Bill and Hil; said Kenny Starr
Had tried to shove her way too far,
Had tried to make her tell a lie.
When she refused to testify
And say what wasn't true was true
Ken did what prosecutors do
And proceeded then to nail her,
Got the fed'ral judge to jail her.
Still Sue refused to say a thing,
Told Kenny Starr she'd never sing.
She never did; they had to free her.
Now walking free these days we see her.
She took the blows and toughed it out.
That Sue's got guts you cannot doubt.
    Of Clinton folks I'm sure no fan,
    But Sue's the best of all that clan.

Defining Moments in History III

Little David took his sling,
Picked up a stone and had his fling
Hit Goliath in the head.
When the giant fell down dead
Dave wound up as Israel's king.

Willie Shakespeare, some folks say,
Never wrote a single play.
Trouble is, the guys that did.
Said, "Let's blame 'em on the kid,"
Which is why Will's great today.

When Jefferson was top banana
He bought from France Louisiana
Though it was not his intent
He wound up with a continent
For which today we shout, "Hosanna!"

Wilbur Wright and Orville, too,
Built a flimsy plane that flew.
Wilbur said to Orville Wright,
"We've just seen the birth of flight.
Now we're headed for the blue."

When the Okies found, too late,
That the dust would not abate
They turned down what fate had dealed,
Drove out west to Bakersfield.
And now they own the Golden State.

O.J. Simpson can't understand
Why he's so roundly, soundly panned
For traveling 'round from town to town,
Hunting his wife's killers down
On every golf course in the land.

Pat Departs

I never thought that I would see
Buchanan leave the GOP.
I never thought that he would go
Join up with nutty Ross Perot,
Not even though there's thirteen mil
That's sitting in Ross's party's till.
I guess it's dough Pat thinks is meant
At last to make him president.
But despite Buchanan's scheming
Most folks know that he's just dreaming.
  When his campaign at last falls flat
  Our Pat may wish that he'd stood pat.

Don't Count Her Out

Now Liddy Dole has left the race,

And done it with aplomb and grace,

She realized that with no dough

President was just no go.

Knew that her dream was pie in sky

So she got out with head held high.

Her race is done but folks will find

She has not left her dreams behind.

She's still got dreams on which to sleep

And one of them is Bush's veep.

There was one Dole and now there's two;

He may have lost but she's not through.

Defining Moments in History IV

Young Arthur pulled the sword from stone,
Then ascended England's throne.
Guinevere saw what he had got,
But still played 'round with Lancelot
And left King Arthur all alone.

Englishmen at last got smarta
And demanded freedom's charta,
Then wrote it down. When they were done
They foisted it on bad King John,
Made him adopt the Magna Carta.

The Frenchmen thought their king was mean,
And held a rally on the green.
Then with just a bit of hassle
Dragged King Louis from his castle
And sliced him with the guillotine.

Darwin thought up evolution,
Started thus a revolution.
But after viewing man and monk
You'd have thought he might have thunk
Up a theory of devolution.

Jimmy Carter from the start
Set himself from us apart.
And so it came as quite a blow
When at last we came to know
That Jimmy lusted in his heart.

The Algore Campaign

There's trouble in Algore's campaign,
(so maybe he's running in vain).
Things are going down hill
And he's off to Nashville.
Is the man completely insane?

And Algore's not raising much dough.
The money is coming in slow.
Bradley is gaining
And Clinton's abstaining –
He working for Hil, don't you know.

Debates are demanded by Gore
To stop Bill Brad at the door.
If the question is who
Is the worst of the two
Debates won't settle the score.

No one's as desperate as Al.
He's called in his tricky old pal,
Slick Tony Coelho,
A dishonest fellow
Who's feasances mostly are mal.

Still Tony is smart as get out
And knows what the game is about,
But helping the Veep
Can't be done on the cheap
It'll cost many millions no doubt.

But Coelho can gather the dough.
He's superb at that, we all know
With Tony at the wheel
He'll beg, borrow or steal
Enough for the campaign to go.

The question is where to begin?
Is Nashville the place to start in?
Is Tony the one
For the victory run
Who'll insure that Algore will win?

Too bad, but time only will tell
If Tony can make the thing jell
Or if Clinton fatigue
Puts him out of his league
And sends poor Algore to hell.

Bill Bradley must certainly hope
That Gore's at the end of his rope
But if he is thinking
That Al will keep sinking,
Like Clinton he's inhaling dope.

Meanwhile Republicans watch
This wonderful Democrat match
And hope when it's over
They'll wind up in clover
And on to the White House they'll latch!

Go, Pat! Go!

So now at last there turns the worm.

Buchanan's gone and joined Reform

He's left the party that he knows

To run with Jesses and Perots,

Also a bunch of other geeks.

Their nomination's what he seeks.

Their nomination and their dough–

The way to go, Pat! Way to go!

Their thirteen mil's just what you need

To make the voters hear and heed

The message that you're sure is meant

To win their votes for president.

The GOP has turned you down.

What you proposed just drew their frown

Their feelings for you are not warm

So, nuts to them, you've joined Reform,

And now you think you're on a roll.

Think with this move you'll reach your goal.

Beware of this, though, as you stump,

You're not alone; there's also Trump.

> Mayhap frustration turned to wrath,
>
> Has led Pat down the primrose path.

103

Cry "Wolf"

While Bill at night is playing golf
Algore, the veep, is crying Wolf.
"Naomi come and help me, please,
And I will pay you 15 Gs
For every month that you're around
To get my campaign off the ground.
Tell me, please, what clothes to wear.
On which side should I part my hair?
Should I wear shoes or cowboy boots?
What color should I buy my suits?
That odd sex stuff you write about –
I think that we can leave it out.
I know you think it might help me,
But I've been taught by Billy C.
Your job? Make me an alpha male.
If you do that I cannot fail."

    While Al may think that's eas'ly done,
    Naomi's task's a daunting one.

Sonnet: To The Leader

He rose up from poverty to bestride
A world beset with fear of strife and war.
His cause was freedom, that had nearly died
Because of timid leaders gone before.
A nation that had once stood strong and tall
Now flinched before the face of tyranny,
'Til he, a leader ans'ring freedom's call,
Began once more the march of liberty.

In lands where freedom only faintly reigned,
Because he dauntless stood and fought for right,
Allies that once had cowardly abstained
Took new courage and joined again the fight.
 Though age now dims his mind of great deeds done
 The world still knows t'was he its freedom won.

The Leader II

I think of things Ron never did:
He never built a pyramid,
He never dammed the Colorado,
Never once misspelled potato
He never dropped the atom bomb,
He never founded Bosch & Lomb
He never freed a single slave.
He won't take millions to his grave
A zillion things he didn't get done.
So why's he rated number one?
He brought the cold war to an end.
Of Gorbachev he made a friend.
And communism he stopped dead,
Thus ending its ongoing spread.
Optimism he brought the land.
Taxes were cut at his demand.
Prosperity he gave the nation,
Brought a halt to long stagflation.
And to our land he brought new pride,
Which some thought had forever died.

    Most men depart without a trace.
    He left the world a better place.

Index of First Lines

ABOUT THE AUTHOR

Lyn Nofziger's career as a Republican political operative grew out of his 16 years as a newspaperman, including eight as Washington correspondent for the Copley Newspapers and News Service. He was Ronald Reagan's press secretary in his first California gubernatorial campaign, and was then Communications Director in the governor's office. Later he was a Deputy Assistant to President Nixon and Deputy Chairman of the Republican National Committee. He was Reagan's press secretary again in Reagan's successful 1980 campaign for the presidency, and was a close political adviser during Reagan's first term. Nofziger has run or participated in numerous political campaigns, including five for president. In addition, he is the author of five Western novels and a political memoir. Lyn's independent and irreverent views, along with poetry written by his alter ego, Joy Skilmer, can be found on the Internet at www.lynnofziger.com.

Photocopy this page

ORDER FORM

To: MND Publishing, Inc.
       573 Marina Road
       Deatsville AL 36022

From: _____

         _____
         _____

         _____

Please send:

#	Unbridled Joy – The Verse of Joy Skilmer		
	Unbridled Joy – The Verse of Joy Skilmer	$14.00	$
	Shipping		
	Total enclosed		

Shipping: $3.50 for first book and $2.00 for each additional book. Please send payment by check (US$ drawn on US bank) or international money order.

❑ Please put me on Lyn's mailing list and send me occasional batches of Joy Skilmer's poetry (free).